Poems By a Little Girl

Hilda Conkling

Contents

POEMS BY A LITTLE GIRL

BY

Hilda Conkling

FOR YOU, MOTHER

I have a dream for you, Mother,
Like a soft thick fringe to hide your eyes.
I have a surprise for you, Mother,
Shaped like a strange butterfly.
I have found a way of thinking
To make you happy;
I have made a song and a poem
All twisted into one.
If I sing, you listen;
If I think, you know.
I have a secret from everybody in the world full of people
But I cannot always remember how it goes;
It is a song
For you, Mother,
With a curl of cloud and a feather of blue
And a mist
Blowing along the sky.
If I sing it some day, under my voice,
Will it make you happy?

Thanks are due to the editors of Poetry: A Magazine of Verse, The
Delineator, Good Housekeeping, The Lyric, St. Nicholas, and Contemporary
Verse for their courteous permission to reprint many of the following
poems.

PREFACE

A book which needs to be written is one dealing with the childhood of authors. It would be not only interesting, but instructive; not merely profitable in a general way, but practical in a particular. We might hope, in reading it, to gain some sort of knowledge as to what environments and conditions are most conducive to the growth of the creative faculty. We might even learn how not to strangle this rare faculty in its early years.

At this moment I am faced with a difficult task, for here is an author and her childhood in a most unusual position; these two conditions--that of being an author, and that of being a child--appear simultaneously, instead of in the due order to which we are accustomed. For I wish at the outset to state, and emphatically, that it is poetry, the stuff and essence of poetry, which this book contains. I know of no other instance in which such really beautiful poetry has been written by a child; but, confronted with so unwonted a state of things, two questions obtrude themselves: how far has the condition of childhood been impaired by, not only the possession, but the expression, of the gift of writing; how far has the condition of authorship (at least in its more mature state still to come) been hampered by this early leap into the light?

The first question concerns the little girl and can best be answered by herself some twenty years hence; the second concerns the world, and again the answer must wait. We can, however, do something--we can see what she is and what she has done. And if the one is interesting to the psychologist, the other is no less important to the poet.

Hilda Conkling is the younger daughter of Mrs. Grace Hazard Conkling, Assistant Professor of English at Smith College, Northampton, Massachusetts. At the time of writing, Hilda has just passed her ninth birthday. Her sister, Elsa, is two years her senior. The children and their mother live all the year round in Northampton, and glimpses of the woods and hills surrounding the little town crop up again and again in these poems. This is Emily Dickinson's country, and there is a reminiscent sameness in the fauna and flora of her poems in these.

The two little girls go to a school a few blocks from where they live. In the afternoons, they take long walks with their mother, or play in the garden while she writes. On rainy days, there are books and Mrs. Conkling's piano, which is not just a piano, for Mrs. Conkling is a musician, and we may imagine that the children hear a special music as they certainly read a special literature. By "special" I do not mean a prescribed course (for dietitians of the mind are quite as apt to be faddists as dietitians of the stomach), but just that sort of reading which a person who passionately loves books would most want to introduce her children to. And here I think we have the answer to the why of Hilda. She and her sister have been their mother's close companions ever since they were born. They have never known that somewhat equivocal relationship--a child with its nurse. They have never been for hours at a time in contact with an elementary intelligence. If Hilda had shown these poems to even the most sympathetic nurse, what would have been the result? In the first place, they would, in all probability, have been lost, since Hilda does not write her poems, but tells them; in the second, they would have been either extravagantly praised or laughingly commented upon. In either case, the fine flower of creation would most certainly have been injured.

Then again, blessed though many of the nurses of childhood undoubtedly are (and we all remember them), they have no means of answering the thousand and one questions of an eager, opening mind. To be an adequate companion to childhood, one must know so many things. Hilda is fortunate in her mother, for if these poems reveal one thing more than another it is that Mrs. Conkling is dowered with an admirable tact. In the dedication poem to her mother, the little girl says:

> "If I sing, you listen;
> If I think, you know."

No finer tribute could be offered by one person to another than the contented certainty of understanding in those two lines.

Hilda tells her poems, and the method of it is this: They come out in the course of conversation, and Mrs. Conkling is so often engaged in writing that there is nothing to be remarked if she scribbles absently while talking to the little girls. But this scribbling is really a complete draught of the poem. Occasionally Mrs. Conkling writes down the poem later from memory and reads it afterwards to the child, who always remembers if it is not exactly in its original form. No line, no cadence, is altered from Hilda's version; the titles have been added for convenience, but they are merely obvious handles derived from the text.

Naturally it is only a small proportion of Hilda's life which is given to poetry. Much is devoted to running about, a part to study, etc. It is, however, significant that Hilda is not very keen about games with other children. Not that she is by any means either shy or solitary, but they do not greatly interest her. Doubtless childhood pays its debt of possession more steadily than we know.

Now to turn to the book itself; at the very start, here is an amazing thing. This slim volume contains one hundred and seven separate poems, and that is counting as one all the very short pieces written between the ages of five and six. Certainly that is a remarkable output for a little girl, and the only possible explanation is that the poems are perfectly instinctive. There is no working over as with an adult poet. Hilda is subconscious, not self-conscious. Her mother says that she rarely hesitates for a word. When the feeling is strong, it speaks for itself. Read the dedication poem, "For You, Mother." It is full of feeling, and of that simple, dignified, adequate diction which is the speech of feeling:

> "I have found a way of thinking
> To make you happy."

That is beautiful, and, once read, inevitable; but it waited for a child to say. Poem after poem is charged with this feeling, this expression of great love:

> "I will sing you a song,
> Sweets-of-my-heart,
> With love in it,
> (How I love you!)"

> "Will you love me to-morrow after next
> As if I had a bird's way of singing?"

But it is not only the pulse of feeling in such passages which makes them surprising; it is the perfectly original expression of it. When one reads a thing and voluntarily exclaims: "How beautiful! How natural! How true!" then one knows that one has stumbled upon that flash of personality which we call genius. These poems are full of such flashes:

> "Sparkle up, little tired flower
> Leaning in the grass!"

. . .

"There is a star that runs very fast,
That goes pulling the moon
Through the tops of the poplars."

. . .

"There is sweetness in the tree,
And fireflies are counting the leaves.
I like this country,
I like the way it has."

A pansy has a "thinking face"; a rooster has a comb "gay as a parade,"
he shouts "crooked words, loud . . . sharp . . . not beautiful!";
frozen water is asked if it cannot "lift" itself "with sun," and "Easter
morning says a glad thing over and over."

No matter who wrote them, those passages would be beautiful, the oldest
poet in the world could not improve upon them; and yet the reader has
only to turn to the text to see the incredibly early age at which such
expressions came into the author's mind.

Where childhood betrays genius is in the mounting up of detail.
Inadequate lines not infrequently jar a total effect, as when, in the
poem of the star pulling the moon, she suddenly ends, "Mr. Moon, does he
make you hurry?" Or, speaking of a drop of water:

"So it went on with its life
For several years
Until at last it was never heard of

Any more."

This is the perennial child, thinking as children think; and we are glad of it. It makes the whole more healthy, more sure of development. When the subconscious mind of Hilda Conkling takes a vacation, she does not "nod," as erstwhile Homer; she merely reverts to type and is a child again.

I think too highly of these poems to speak of the volume as though it were the finished achievement of a grown-up person. Some of the poems can be taken in that way, but by no means all. The child who writes them frequently transcends herself, but her thoughts for the most part are those proper to every imaginative child. Fairies play a large role in her fancies, and so does the sandman. There are kings, and princesses, and golden wings, and there are reminiscences of story-books, and hints of pictures that have pleased her. After all, that is the way we all make our poems, but the grown-up poet tries to get away from his author, he tries to see more than the painter has seen. The little girl is quite untroubled by any questions of technique. She takes what to her is the obvious always, and in these copied pieces it is, naturally, less her own peculiar obvious than in the nature poems.

Hilda Conkling is evidently possessed of a rare and accurate power of observation. And when we add this to her gift of imagination, we see that it is the perfectly natural play of these two faculties which makes what to her is an obvious expression. She does not search for it, it is her natural mode of thought. But, luckily for her, she has been guided by a wisdom which has not attempted to show her a better way. Her observation has been carefully, but unobtrusively, cultivated; her imagination has been stimulated by the reading of excellent books; but both these lines of instruction have been kept apparently apart from her own work. She has been let alone there; she has been taught by an analogy which she has never suspected. By this means, her poetical gift has functioned happily, without ever for a moment experiencing the tension of doubt.

A few passages will serve to show how well Hilda knows how to use her eyes:

> "The water came in with a wavy look
> Like a spider's web."

A bluebird has a back "like a feathered sky." Apostrophizing a snow-capped mountain she writes:

> "You shine like a lily
> But with a different whiteness."

She asks a humming-bird:

> "Why do you stand on the air
> And no sun shining?"

She hears a chickadee:

> "Far off I hear him talking
> The way smooth bright pebbles
> Drop into water."

Now let us follow her a step farther, to where the imagination takes a firmer hold:

> "The world turns softly
> Not to spill its lakes and rivers.
> The water is held in its arms
> And the sky is held in the water."

School lessons, and a reflection in a pond--that is the stuff of which all poetry is made. It is the fusion which shows the quality of the poet. Turn to the text and read "Geography." Really, this is an extraordinary child!

It is pleasant to watch her with the artist's eagerness intrigued by the sounds of words, for instance:

"--silvery lonesome lapping of the long wave."

Again, enchanted by a little bell of rhyme, we have this amusing catalogue:

"John-flowers,
Mary-flowers,
Polly-flowers
Cauli-flowers."

That is the conscious Hilda, the gay little girl, but it shows a quick ear nevertheless. We can almost hear the giggle with which that "Cauliflowers" came out. Usually rhyme does not appear to be a matter of moment to her. Some poets think in rhyme, some do not; Hilda evidently belongs to the second category. "Treasure," and "The Apple-Jelly-Fish-Tree," and "Short Story" are the only poems in the book which seem to follow a clearly rhymed pattern. If any misguided schoolmistress had ever suggested that a poem should have rhyme and metre, this book would never have been "told." In "Moon Doves," however, there is a distinctly metrical effect without rhyme. But the great majority of the poems are built upon cadence, and the subtlety of this little girl's cadences are a delight to those who can hear them. Doubtless her musical inheritance has all to do with this, for in poem after poem the instinct for rhythm is unerring. So constantly is this the case, that it is scarcely necessary to point out particular examples. I may, however, name, as two of her best for other qualities as well, "Gift," and "Poems." The latter contains two of her quick strokes of observation and comparison: the morning "like the inside of a snow-apple," and she herself curled "cushion-shaped" in the window-seat.

Dear me! How simple these poems seem when you read them done. But try to write something new about a dandelion. Try it; and then read the poem of that name here. It is charming; how did she think of it? How indeed!

Delightful conceits she has--another is "Sun Flowers"--but how comes a child of eight to prick and point with the rapier of irony? For it is nothing less than irony in "The Tower and the Falcon." Did she quite grasp its meaning herself? We may doubt it. In this poem, the subconscious is very much on the job.

To my thinking, the most successful poems in the book--and now I mean successful from a grown-up standpoint--are "For You, Mother," "Red Rooster," "Gift," "Poems," "Dandelion," "Butterfly," "Weather," "Hills," and "Geography." And it will be noticed that these are precisely the poems which must have sprung from actual experience. They are not the book poems, not even the fairy poems, they are the records of reactions from actual happenings. I have not a doubt that Hilda prefers her fairy-stories. They are the conscious play of her imagination, it must be "fun" to make them. Ah, but it is the unconscious with which we are most concerned, those very poems which are probably to her the least interesting are the ones which most certainly reveal the fulness of poetry from which she draws. She probably hardly thought at all, so natural was it, to say that three pinks "smell like more of them in a blue vase," but the expression fills the air with so strong a scent that no superlative could increase it.

"Gift" is a lovely poem, it has feeling, expression, originality, cadence. If a child can write such a poem at eight years old, what does it mean? That depends, I think, on how long the instructors of youth can be persuaded to keep "hands off." A period of imitation is, I fear, inevitable, but if consciousness is not induced by direct criticism, if instruction in the art of writing is abjured, the imitative period will probably be got through without undue loss. I think there is too much native sense of beauty and proportion here to be entirely killed even by the drying and freezing process which goes by the name of education.

What this book chiefly shows is high promise; but it also has its pages of real achievement, and that of so high an order it may well set us pondering.

AMY LOWELL.

FOUR TO FIVE YEARS OLD

FIRST SONGS

I
Rosy plum-tree, think of me
When Spring comes down the world!

II
There's dozens full of dandelions
Down in the field:
Little gold plates,
Little gold dishes in the grass.
I cannot count them,
But the fairies know every one.

III
Oh wrinkling star, wrinkling up so wise,
When you go to sleep do you shut your eyes?

IV
The red moon comes out in the night.
When I'm asleep, the moon comes pattering up
Into the trees.
Then I peep out my window
To watch the moon go by.

V

Sparkle up, little tired flower
Leaning in the grass!
Did you find the rain of night
Too heavy to hold?

VI

The garden is full of flowers
All dancing round and round.
    John-flowers,
    Mary-flowers,
    Polly-flowers,
    Cauli-flowers,
They dance round and round
And they bow down and down
To a black-eyed daisy.

VII

There is going to be the sound of bells
And murmuring.
This is the brook dance:
There is going to be sound of voices,
And the smallest will be the brook:
It is the song of water
You will hear,
A little winding song
To dance to . . .

VIII

Blossoms in the growing tree,
Why don't you speak to me?
I want to grow like you,
Smiling . . . smiling . . .

IX

If I find a moon,
I will sing a moon-song.
If I find a flower,
What song shall I sing,
Rose-song or clover-song?

X

The blossoms will be gone in the winter:
Oh apples, come for the June!
Can you come, will you bloom?
Will you stay till the cold?

XI

I will sing you a song,
Sweets-of-my-heart,
With love in it,
(How I love you!)
And a rose to swing in the wind,
The wind that swings roses!

XII

Will you love me to-morrow after next,
As if I had a bird's way of singing?

GARDEN OF THE WORLD

The butterfly swings over the violet
That stands by the water,
In the garden that sings
All day.
The sun goes up in the dawn,
The water waves softly.
In the trees are little breezes,
In the garden trees.
Blue hills and blue waters I
The big blue ocean lies around in the sun
Watching his waves toss . . .

THEATRE-SONG

Eagles were flying over the sky
And mermaids danced in the gold waters.
Eagles were calling over the sky
And the water was the color of blue flowers.

Sunshine was 'flected in the waves
Like meadows of white buds.
This is what I saw
On a morning long ago . . .

VELVETS

By a Bed of Pansies

This pansy has a thinking face
Like the yellow moon.
This one has a face with white blots:
I call him the clown.
Here goes one down the grass
With a pretty look of plumpness;
She is a little girl going to school
With her hands in the pockets of her pinafore.
Her name is Sue.
I like this one, in a bonnet,
Waiting,

Her eyes are so deep!
But these on the other side,
These that wear purple and blue,
They are the Velvets,
The king with his cloak,
The queen with her gown,
The prince with his feather.
These are dark and quiet
And stay alone.

I know you, Velvets,
Color of Dark,
Like the pine-tree on the hill
When stars shine!

TWO SONGS

After Hearing the Wagner Story-book

The birds came to tell Siegfried a story,
A story of the woods out of a tree:
How the ring was fairy
And there were things it could do for him
Day and night:
How the river flowed green and wavy
Under the Rainbow Bridge,
And Brunnhilda slept in a wreath of fire.
Grane watched her, standing close beside,
Grane the big white horse,
Dear Grane of her heart.
She dreamed she was far from her father,
But Siegfried was coming,
Siegfried, through the big trees,
Up the hill,
Through the fire!

II

"Siegfried, hear us!
Give us back the ring!"
The lady with the shell,
The water-lady with the green hair,
Calling, cried "Siegfried!"
But he laughed to hear her,
Laughed in the sun
And went into the woods laughing:
He was happy in his heart,
And he had golden hair
Till the sun loved him.
"Siegfried!"
I will call him!
"Siegfried!"
But he will not hear me.
He could talk to birds and rivers,
And he is gone.

MOON SONG

There is a star that runs very fast,
That goes pulling the moon
Through the tops of the poplars.
It is all in silver,
The tall star:
The moon rolls goldenly along

Out of breath.
Mr. Moon, does he make you hurry?

SUNSET

Once upon a time at evening-light
A little girl was sad.
There was a color in the sky,
A color she knew in her dreamful heart
And wanted to keep.
She held out her arms
Long, long,
And saw it flow away on the wind.
When it was gone
She did not love the moonlight
Or care for the stars.
She had seen the rose in the sky.

Sometimes I am sad
Because I have a thought
Of this little girl.

MOUSE

Little mouse in gray velvet,
Have you had a cheese-breakfast?
There are no crumbs on your coat,
Did you use a napkin?
I wonder what you had to eat,
And who dresses you in gray velvet?

SHORT STORY

I found the gold on the hill;
I found the hid gold!

The wicked queen
Stole the gold,
Hid it under a stone
And never told.

The selfish queen
Rolling away
In her white limousine,
Never knew nor dreamed
That I searched all day
Till I found the gold,
The gold!

BY LAKE CHAMPLAIN

I was bare as a leaf
And I felt the wind on my shoulder.
The trees laughed
When I picked up the sun in my fingers.
The wind was chasing the waves,
Tangling their white curls.
"Willow trees," I said,
"O willows,
Look at your lake!
Stop laughing at a little girl
Who runs past your feet in the sand!"

SPRING SONG

I love daffodils.
I love Narcissus when he bends his head.
I can hardly keep March and spring and Sunday and daffodils
Out of my rhyme of song.
Do you know anything about the spring
When it comes again?
God knows about it while winter is lasting.
Flowers bring him power in the spring,
And birds bring it, and children.
He is sometimes sad and alone
Up there in the sky trying to keep his worlds happy.
I bring him songs

When he is in his sadness, and weary.
I tell him how I used to wander out
To study stars and the moon he made,
And flowers in the dark of the wood.
I keep reminding him about his flowers he has forgotten,
And that snowdrops are up.
What can I say to make him listen?
"God," I say,
"Don't you care!
Nobody must be sad or sorry
In the spring-time of flowers."

WATER

The world turns softly
Not to spill its lakes and rivers.
The water is held in its arms
And the sky is held in the water.
What is water,
That pours silver,
And can hold the sky?

SHADY BRONN

When the clouds come deep against the sky
I sit alone in my room to think,

To remember the fairy dreams I made,
Listening to the rustling out of the trees.
The stories in my fairy-tale book
Come new to me every day.
But at my farm on the hill-top
I have the wind for a fairy,
And the shapes of things:
Shady Bronn is the name of my little farm:
It is the name of a dream I have
Where leaves move,
And the wind rings them like little bells.

CHICKADEE

The chickadee in the appletree
Talks all the time very gently.
He makes me sleepy.
I rock away to the sea-lights.
Far off I hear him talking
The way smooth bright pebbles
Drop into water . . .
Chick-a-dee-dee-dee . . .

THE CHAMPLAIN SANDMAN

The Sandman comes pattering across the Bay:
His hair is silver,
His footstep soft.
The moon shines on his silver hair,
On his quick feet.
The Sandman comes searching across the Bay:
He goes to all the houses he knows
To put sand in little girls' eyes.
That is why I go to my sleepy bed,
And why the lake-gull leaves the moon alone.
There are no wings to moonlight any more,
Only the Sandman's hair.

ROSE-MOSS

Little Rose-moss beside the stone,
Are you lonely in the garden?
There are no friends of you,
And the birds are gone.
Shall I pick you?"

"Little girl up by the hollyhock,
I am not lonely.
I feel the sun burning,
I hold light in my cup,
I have all the rain I want,

I think things to myself that you don't know,
And I listen to the talk of crickets.
I am not lonely,
But you may pick me
And take me to your mother."

ABOUT MY DREAMS

Now the flowers are all folded
And the dark is going by.
The evening is arising . . .
It is time to rest.
When I am sleeping
I find my pillow full of dreams.
They are all new dreams:
No one told them to me
Before I came through the cloud.
They remember the sky, my little dreams,
They have wings, they are quick, they are sweet.
Help me tell my dreams
To the other children,
So that their bread may taste whiter,
So that the milk they drink
May make them think of meadows
In the sky of stars.
Help me give bread to the other children
So that their dreams may come back:
So they will remember what they knew
Before they came through the cloud.
Let me hold their little hands in the dark,
The lonely children,

ABOUT MY DREAMS

The babies that have no mothers any more.
Dear God, let me hold up my silver cup
For them to drink,
And tell them the sweetness
Of my dreams.

AUTUMN SONG

I made a ring of leaves
On the autumn grass:
I was a fairy queen all day.
Inside the ring, the wind wore sandals
Not to make a noise of going.
The caterpillars, like little snow men,
Had wound themselves in their winter coats.
The hands of the trees were bare
And their fingers fluttered.
I was a queen of yellow leaves and brown,
And the redness of my fairy ring
Kept me warm.
For the wind blew near,
Though he made no noise of going,
And I hadn't a close-made wrap
Like the caterpillars.
Even a queen of fairies can be cold
When summer has forgotten and gone!
Keep me warm, red leaves;
Don't let the frost tiptoe into my ring
On the magic grass!

THE DREAM

When I slept, I thought I was upon the mountain-tops,
And this is my dream.
I saw the little people come out into the night,
I saw their wings glittering under the stars.
Crickets played all the tunes they knew.
It was so comfortable with light . . .
Stars, a rainbow, the moon!
The fairies had shiny crowns
On their bright hair.
The bottoms of their little gowns were roses!
It was musical in the moony light,
And the fairy queen,
Oh, it was all golden where she came
With tiny pages on her trail.
She walked slowly to her high throne,
Slowly, slowly to music,
And watched the dancing that went on
All night long in star-glitter
On the mountain-tops.

BUTTERFLY

Butterfly,
I like the way you wear your wings.
Show me their colors,
For the light is going.
Spread out their edges of gold,
Before the Sandman puts me to sleep
And evening murmurs by.

EVENING

Now it is dusky,
And the hermit thrush and the black and white warbler
Are singing and answering together.
There is sweetness in the tree,
And fireflies are counting the leaves.
I like this country,
I like the way it has,
But I cannot forget my dream I had of the sea,
The gulls swinging and calling,
And the foamy towers of the waves.

THUNDER SHOWER

The dark cloud raged.
Gone was the morning light.
The big drops darted down:
The storm stood tall on the rose-trees:
And the bees that were getting honey
Out of wet roses,
The hiding bees would not come out of the flowers
Into the rain.

RED CROSS SONG

When I heard the bees humming in the hive,
They were so busy about their honey,
I said to my mother,
What can I give,
What can I give to help the Red Cross?
And Mother said to me:
You can give honey too!
Honey of smiles!
Honey of love!

PURPLE ASTERS

It isn't alone the asters
In my garden,
It is the butterflies gleaming
Like crowns of kings and queens!
It isn't alone purple
And blue on the edge of purple,
It is what the sun does,
And the air moving clearly,
The petals moving and the wings,
In my queer little garden!

SONG FOR A PLAY

Soldier drop that golden spear!
Wait till the fires arise!
Wait till the sky drops down and touches the spear,
Crystal and mother-of-pearl!
The sunlight droops forward
Like wings.
The birds sing songs of sun-drops.
The sky leans down where the spear stands upward. . .
I hear music . . .
It is the end . . .

PEACOCK FEATHERS

On trees of fairyland
Grow peacock feathers of daylight colors
Like an Austrian fan.
But there is a strange thing!
I have heard that night gathers these feathers
For her cloak;
I have heard that the stars, the moon,
Are the eyes of peacock feathers
From fairy trees.
It is a thing that may be,
But I should not be sure of it, my dear,
If I were you!

RED ROOSTER

Red rooster in your gray coop,
O stately creature with tail-feathers red and blue,
Yellow and black,
You have a comb gay as a parade
On your head:
You have pearl trinkets
On your feet:
The short feathers smooth along your back
Are the dark color of wet rocks,
Or the rippled green of ships
When I look at their sides through water.

I don't know how you happened to be made
So proud, so foolish,
Wearing your coat of many colors,
Shouting all day long your crooked words,
Loud . . . sharp . . . not beautiful!

TREE-TOAD

Tree-toad is a small gray person
With a silver voice.
Tree-toad is a leaf-gray shadow
That sings.
Tree-toad is never seen
Unless a star squeezes through the leaves,
Or a moth looks sharply at a gray branch.
How would it be, I wonder,
To sing patiently all night,
Never thinking that people are asleep?
Raindrops and mist, starriness over the trees,
The moon, the dew, the other little singers,
Cricket . . . toad . . . leaf rustling . . .
They would listen:
It would be music like weather
That gets into all the corners
Of out-of-doors.

Every night I see little shadows
I never saw before.
Every night I hear little voices
I never heard before.

When night comes trailing her starry cloak,
I start out for slumberland,
With tree-toads calling along the roadside.
Good-night, I say to one, Good-by, I say to another:
I hope to find you on the way
We have traveled before!
I hope to hear you singing on the Road of Dreams!

SEVEN TO NINE YEARS OLD

THE LONESOME WAVE

There is an island
In the middle of my heart,
And all day comes lapping on the shore
A long silver wave.
It is the lonesome wave;
I cannot see the other side of it.
It will never go away
Until it meets the glad gold wave
Of happiness!

Wandering over the monstrous rocks,
Looking into the caves,
I see my island dark, all cold,
Until the gold wave sweeps in
From a sea deep blue,
And flings itself on the beach.
Oh, it is joy, then!
No more whispers like sorrow,
No more silvery lonesome lapping of the long wave . . .

RED-CAP MOSS

Have you seen red-cap moss
In the woods?
Have you looked under the trembling caps
For faces?
Have you seen wonder on those faces
Because you are so big?

RAMBLER ROSE

Rambler Rose in great clusters,
Looking at me, at my mother with me
Under this apple-tree,
Your faces watch us from outside the shade.
   The wind blows on you,
   The rain drops on you,
   The sun shines on you,
You are brighter than before.
You turn your faces to the wind
And watch my mother and me,
Thinking of things I cannot mention
Outside of my mind.
Rambler Rose in the shining wind,
You smile at me,
Smile at my mother!

GIFT

This is mint and here are three pinks
I have brought you, Mother.
They are wet with rain
And shining with it.
The pinks smell like more of them
In a blue vase:
The mint smells like summer
In many gardens.

THE WHITE CLOUD

There are many clouds
But not like the one I see,
For mine floats like a swan in featheriness
Over the River of the Broken Pine.

There are many clouds
But not like the one that goes sailing
Like a ship full of gold that shines,
Like a ship leaning above blue water.

There are many clouds
But not like the one I wait for,
For mine will have a strangeness
Whiter than anything your eyes remember.

MOON THOUGHT

The moon is thinking of the river
Winding through the mountains far away,
Because she has a river in her heart
Full of the same silver.

THE OLD BRIDGE

The old bridge has a wrinkled face.
He bends his back
For us to go over.
He moans and weeps
But we do not hear.
Sorrow stands in his face
For the heavy weight and worry
Of people passing.
The trees drop their leaves into the water;
The sky nods to him.
The leaves float down like small ships
On the blue surface
Which is the sky.
He is not always sad:
He smiles to see the ships go down
And the little children
Playing on the river banks.

FERNS

Small ferns up-coming through the mossy green,
Up-curling and springing,
See trees circling round them,
And the straight brook like a lily-stem:
Hear the water laughing
At the stern old pine-tree
Who keeps sighing to himself all day long
What's the use! What's the use!

LAND OF NOD

I wander mountain to mountain,
From sea to sea,
I wander into a country
Where everyone is asleep.
There in the Land of Nod
I never think of home,
For home is there,
With sleeping doves and silvery girls,
Sleeping boys and drowsy roses.
There I find people whose eyes are heavy,
And trees with folded wings.

SUN FLOWERS

Sun-flowers, stop growing!
If you touch the sky where those clouds are passing
Like tufts of dandelion gone to seed,
The sky will put you out!
You know it is blue like the sea . . .
Maybe it is wet, too!
Your gold faces will be gone forever
If you brush against that blue
Ever so softly!

HOLLAND SONG

For a Dutch picture

When light comes creeping through the
That shine with mist,
When winds blow soft,
Windmills wake and whirl.
In Holland, in Holland,
Everything is cheerful
Across the sea:
White nets are beside the water
Where ships sail by.
The mountains begin to get blue,
The Dutch girls begin to sing,
The windmills begin to whirl.

Then night comes
The mountains turn dark gray
And faint away into night.
Not a bird chirps his song.
All is drowsy,
All is strange,
With the moon and stars shining round the world:
The wind stops,
The windmills stop
In Holland . . .

FOUNTAIN-TALK

Said the fountain to its clear bed,
"You might flow faster!
I am sprinkling my best, every day,
But ice is holding you fast.
Can't you get out?
Can't you lift yourself with sun?
I am tired waiting for slow cold water
To fling about the air:
Can't you wake yourself up?"
But the fountain-basin murmured softly
"Sleep . . . sleep . . .
Sleep . . . sleep . . .
You with your talking and talking!
Hush . . . hush . . .
I hear the bird-sandman!"

POPLARS

The poplars bow forward and back;
They are like a fan waving very softly.
They tremble,
For they love the wind in their feathery branches.
They love to look down at the shallows,
    At the mermaids
    On the sandy shore;
They love to look into morning's face
    Cool in the water.

THE TOWER AND THE FALCON

There was a tower, once,
In a London street.
It was the highest, widest, thickest tower,
The proudest, roundest, finest tower
Of all towers.
English men passed it by:
They could not see it all
Because it went above tree-tops and clouds.

It was lonely up there where the trees stopped
Until one day
A blue falcon came flying.
He cried:
"Tower! Do you know you are the highest, finest, roundest,

The tallest, proudest, greatest,
Of all the towers
In all the world?"

He went away.
That night the tower made a new song
About himself.

THOUGHTS

My thoughts keep going far away
Into another country under a different sky:
My thoughts are sea-foam and sand;
They are apple-petals fluttering.

POEM-SKETCH IN THREE PARTS

(Made for the picture on the jacket of the
Norwegian book, The Great Hunger, by Johan Bojer)

I
THE ROLLING IN OF THE WAVE

It was night when the sky was dark blue
And the water came in with a wavy look
Like a spider's web.
The point of the slope came down to the water's edge;
It was green with a fairy ring of forget-me-not and fern.
The white foam licked the side of the slope
As it came up and bent backward;
It curled up like a beautiful cinder-tree
Bending in the wind.

II
THE COMING OF THE GREAT BIRD

A boy was watching the water
As it came lapping the edge of fern.
Little ships passed him
As the moon came leaning across dark blue rays of light.
The spruce trees saw the white ships sailing away,
And the moon bending up the blue sky
Where stars were twinkling like fairy lamps;
The boy was looking toward foreign lands
As the ships passed,
Their white sails glittering in the moonlight.
He was thinking how he wished to see
Foreign lands, strange people,
When suddenly a bird came flying!
It swooped down upon the slope
And spoke to him:
"Do you want to go across the deep blue sea?
Get on my back; I will take you."
"Oh," cried the little boy, "who sent you?
Who knew my thoughts of foreign lands?"

III
THE ISLAND

They flew as the night-wind flowed, very softly,
They heard sweet singing that the water sang,
They came to a place where the sea was shallow
And saw treasure hidden there.
There was one poplar tree
On the lonely island,
Swaying for sadness.
The clouds went over their heads
Like a fleet of drifting ships.
And there they sank down out of the air
Into the dream.

THE DEW-LIGHT

The Dew-man comes over the mountains wide,
Over the deserts of sand,
With his bag of clear drops
And his brush of feathers.
He scatters brightness.
The white bunnies beg him for dew.
He sprinkles their fur,
They shake themselves.
All the time he is singing
    The unknown world is beautiful!

He polishes flowers,
Humming "Oh, beautiful!"
He sings in the soft light
That grows out of the dew,
Out of the misty dew-light that leans over him
He makes his song . . .
    It is beautiful, the unknown world!

YELLOW SUMMER-THROAT

Yellow summer-throat sat singing
In a bending spray of willow tree.
Thin fine green-y lines on his throat,
The ruffled outside of his throat,
Trembled when he sang.
He kept saying the same thing;
The willow did not mind.

    I knew what he said, I knew,
    But how can I tell you?

I have to watch the willow bend in the wind.

PEGASUS

Come dear Pegasus, I said,
Let me ride on your back;
I have often seen your shadow in the glittering creek;
Pegasus, beautiful Pegasus,
Let me sit on your back!

He was away,
But I was on his back,
So I went with him.
We had a castle in a mountain cloud.
So quickly was he away,
I had no time to look or speak!
That was the last I saw of father or mother.
We went far from the shining creek,
Farther than I know how to tell you:
It was good-by.

VENICE BRIDGE

For a painting

Away back in an old city
I saw a bridge.
That bridge belonged to Venice.
It was to the rainbow clear
It traveled,

Over an old canal.
You had to pass a cloudy gate
To reach the color . . .
Bridges do sometimes begin on the earth
And end in the sky.

NIGHT GOES RUSHING BY

Night goes hurrying over
Like sweeping clouds;
The birds are nested; their song is silent.
The wind says oo--oo--oo--through the trees
For their lullaby.
The moon shines down on the sleeping birds.

My cottage roof is like a sheet of silk
Spun like a cobweb.
My apple-trees are bare as the oaks in the forest;
When the moon shines
I see no leaves.

I am alone and very quiet
Hoping the moon may say something
Before long.

DANDELION

O little soldier with the golden helmet,
What are you guarding on my lawn?
You with your green gun
And your yellow beard,
Why do you stand so stiff?
There is only the grass to fight!

IF I COULD TELL YOU THE WAY

Down through the forest to the river
I wander.
There are swans flying,
Swans on the water,
Duck, wild birds.
Fairies live here;
They know no sorrow.
Birds, winds,
They are the only people.
If I could tell you the way to this place,
You would sell your house and your land
For silver or a little gold,
You would sail up the river,
Tie your boat to the Black Stone,
Build a leaf-hut, make a twig-fire,
Gather mushrooms, drink spring-water,
Live alone and sing to yourself
For a year and a year and a year!

ROSE-PETAL

Petal with rosy cheeks,
Petal with thoughts of your own,
Petal of my crimson-white flower out of June,
Little petal of my heart!

POEMS

See the fur coats go by!
The morning is like the inside of a snow-apple.
I will curl myself cushion-shape
On the window-seat;
I will read poems by snow-light.
If I cannot understand them so,
I will turn them upside down
And read them by the red candles
Of garden brambles.

SEAGARDE

I will return to you
O stillest and dearest,
To see the pearl of light
That flashes in your golden hair;

To hear you sing your songs of starlight
And tell your stories of the wonderful land
Of stars and fleecy sky;
To say to you that Seagarde will soon be here,
Seagarde the fairy
With her seagulls of hope!

EASTER

On Easter morn
Up the faint cloudy sky
I hear the Easter bell,
Ding dong . . . ding dong . . .
Easter morning scatters lilies
On every doorstep;
Easter morning says a glad thing
Over and over.
Poor people, beggars, old women
Are hearing the Easter bell . . .
Ding dong . . . ding dong . . .

BLUEBIRD

Oh bluebird with light red breast,
And your blue back like a feathered sky,
You have to go down south
Before biting winter comes
And my flower-beds are covered with fluff out of the clouds.
Before you go,
Sing me one more song
Of tree-tops down south,
Of darkies singing their babies to sleep,
Of sand and glittering stones
Where rivers pass;
Then . . . good-by!

GEOGRAPHY

I can tell balsam trees
By their grayish bluish silverish look of smoke.
Pine trees fringe out.
Hemlocks look like Christmas.
The spruce tree is feathered and rough
Like the legs of the red chickens in our poultry yard.
I can study my geography from chickens
Named for Plymouth Rock and Rhode Island,
And from trees out of Canada.
No; I shall leave the chickens out.
I shall make a new geography of my own.

I shall have a hillside of spruce and hemlock
Like a separate country,
And I shall mark a walk of spires on my map,
A secret road of balsam trees
With blue buds.
Trees Fat smell like a wind out of fairy-land
Where little people live
Who need no geography
But trees.

MARCH THOUGHT

I am waiting for the flowers
To come back:
I am alone,
But I can wait for the birds.

MORNING

There is a brook I must hear
Before I go to sleep.
There is a birch tree I must visit
Every night of clearness.
I have to do some dreaming,
I have to listen a great deal,
Before light comes back

By a silver arrow of cloud,
And I rub my eyes and say
It must be morning on this hill!

SONG

A scarlet bird went sailing away through the wood . . .

It was only a mist of dream
That floated by.

Bare boughs of my apple-tree,
Beautiful gray arms stretched out to me,
Swaying to and fro like angels' wings . . .

It was only a mist of dream
That floated by.

SNOWFLAKE SONG

Snowflakes come in fleets
Like ships over the sea.
The moon shines down on the crusty snow:
The stars make the sky sparkle like gold-fish
In a glassy bowl.
Bluebirds are gone now,

But they left their song behind them.
The moon seems to say:
It is time for summer when the birds come back
To pick up their lonesome songs.

SNOWSTORM

Snowflakes are dancing.
They run down out of heaven.
Coming home from somewhere down the long tired road
They flake us sometimes
The way they do the grass,
And the stretch of the world.
The grass-blades are crowned with snowflakes.
They make me think of daisies
With white frills around their necks
With golden faces and green gowns;
Poor little daisies,
Tip-toe and shivering
In the cold!

POPPY

Oh big red poppy,
You look stern and sturdy,
Yet you bow to the wind
And sing a lullaby . . .
    "Sleep, little ones under my breast
    In the moonshine . . ."
You make this lullaby,
Sweet, short,
Slow, beautiful,
And you thank the dew for giving you a drink.

BUTTERFLY

As I walked through my garden
I saw a butterfly light on a flower.
His wings were pink and purple:
He spoke a small word . . .
It was Follow!
"I cannot follow"
I told him,
"I have to go the opposite way."

CLOUDS

The clouds were gray all day.
At last they departed
And the blue diamonds shone again.
I watched clouds float past and flow back
Like waves across the sea,
Waves that are foamy and soft,
When they hear clouds calling
Mother Sea, send us up your song
Of hushaby!

NARCISSUS

Narcissus, I like to watch you grow
When snow is shining
Beyond the crystal glass.
A coat of snow covers the hills far.
The sun is setting;
And you stretch out flowers of palest white
In the pink of the sun.

LITTLE SNAIL

I saw a little snail
Come down the garden walk.
He wagged his head this way . . . that way . . .
Like a clown in a circus.
He looked from side to side
As though he were from a different country.
I have always said he carries his house on his back . . .
To-day in the rain
I saw that it was his umbrella!

CHERRIES ARE RIPE

The cherry tree is red now;
Cherry tree nods his red head
And calls to the sun:
Let down the birds out of the sky;
Send home the birds to build nests in my arms,
For I am ready to feed them.
There is a little girl coming for cherries too . . .
(I am that little girl, I who am singing . . .)
She is coming with hair flying!
The butterflies will be going (says the cherry)
For it is getting dusk.
When it is dawn,
They will be up and out with the dew,
And sparkle as the dew does

On the tips of tall slender green grasses
Around my feet,
Or on the cheeks of fruit I have ripened,
Red cherries for birds
And children.

A THING FORGOTTEN

White owl is not gloomy;
Black bat is not sad.
It is only that each has forgotten
Something he used to remember:
Black bat goes searching . . . searching . . .
White owl says over and over
Who? What? Where?

LITTLE PAPOOSE:

Little papoose
swung high in the branches
Hears a song of birds, stars, clouds,
Small nests of birds,
Small buds of flowers.
But he is thinking of his mother with dark hair
Like her horse's mane.

Fair clouds nod to him
Where he swings in the tree,
But he is thinking of his father

Dark and glistening and wonderful,
Of his father with a voice like ice and velvet,
And tones of falling water,
Of his father who shouts
Like a storm.

FAIRIES AGAIN

Fairies dancing in the woods at night
Make me think of foreign places,
Of places unknown.
Fairies with sparkling crowns and dewy hands,
Sprinkle flowers and mosses to keep them fresh,
Talk to the birds to keep them cheery.
Once a bird came home
And found a fairy asleep in his nest,
Upon his baby eggs,
To keep them warm!

OH, MY HAZEL-EYED MOTHER

Oh, my hazel-eyed mother,
I looked behind the mulberry bush
And saw you standing there.
You were all in white
With a star on your forehead.

Oh, my hazel-eyed mother,
I do not remember what you said to me,
But the light floating above you
Was your love for your little girl.

THE GREEN PALM TREE

I sat under a delicate palm tree
On a shore of sounding waves.
I felt sure I was alone,
Listening.
    A sea-gull flew by from France,
    A sea-gull flew by from Spain,
    A sea-gull flew by from Mexico!
I laughed softly
When they saw me:
It was those travelers
From foreign countries
Changed my thoughts
To laughter!

TREASURE

Robbers carry a treasure
Into a field of wheat.
With a great bag of silk
They go on careful feet.
They dig a hole, deep, deep,
They bury it under a stone,
Cover it up with turf,
Leave it alone.
What is there in the bag?
Stones that shine, gold?
_I_ cannot rob the robbers!
THEY have not told.
To-night I'd like to know
If they will go
Softly to find the treasure?
I'd like to know
How much yellow gold
A bag like that can hold?

TWO PICTURES

I

Gorgeous Blue Mountain

I see a great mountain
Stand among clouds;
You would never know
Where it ended. . . .
Oh, gorgeous blue mountain of my heart
And of my love for you!

II

Sea-Gull

From a yellow strip of sand
I watch a gull go by.
He is bright-eyed
To see the world of waves.
All his dream is of the sea.
All his love is for his mate.

TELL ME

Tell me quiet things
When it is shadowy:
It is at morningbreak you must tell me tales
Like those about Odysseus,
Morning is the time for ships
And strangers!

SILVERHORN

It is out in the mountains
I find him,
My snowy deer
With silver horns like dew,
Horns that sparkle.
I think I see him in the hollow,
He is on the high hill!
I think I see him on the hill,
He is leaping through the air!
I think I can ride upon his back,
He is like moonlight I cannot hold,
He is like thoughts I lose.
He flows by
All white . . .
He makes me think of the brook
Out of the hills
With its little foamy points

Like his twitching ears,
Like his horns of silver
Sparkling.

The brook is his only friend
When he travels . . .
Silverhorn, Silverhorn!

SPARKLING DROP OF WATER

The sun shone,

All was still.
The sun made one sparkle in one drop
Before it fell
Down into the mossy green
That was the grass.
It lay there silent
A long time.
The sun went, the moon came,
Again one sparkle in the grass!
Day then night, sun then moon,
Year in, year out,
So it went on with its life
For several years
Until at last it was never heard of
Any more.

HAY-COCK

This is another kind of sweetness
Shaped like a bee-hive:
This is the hive the bees have lefts
It is from this clover-heap
They took away the honey
For the other hive!

ONLY MORNING-GLORY THAT FLOWERED

Under the vine I saw one morning-glory
A tight unfolding bud
Half out.
He looked hard down into my lettuce-bed.
He was thinking hard.
He said I want a friend!
I was standing there:
I said, Well, I am here! Don't you see me?
But he thought and thought.

The next day I found him happy,
Quite out,
Looking about the world.
The wind blew sweet airs,
Carried away his perfume in the sun;
And near by swung a new flower
Uncurling its hands . . .

He was not thoughtful
Any more!

WEATHER

Weather is the answer
When I can't go out into flowery places;
Weather is my wonder
About the kind of morning
Hidden behind the hills of sky.

SUMMER-DAY SONG

Wild birds fly over me.
I am not the blue curtain overhead,
I am the one who lives under the sky.
I swing to the tree-tops,
I pick strawberries,
I sing and play,
And happiness makes me like a great god
On the earth.
It makes me think of great things
A little girl like me
Could not know of.

PINK ROSE-PETALS

Pink rose-petals
Fluttering down in hosts,
I know what you mean
Sometimes, in Spring.
It is love you mean.

Love has a gray bird
That flutters down;
A dove that comes flying
Saying the same thing.

How happy it makes me to think of it,
Rose-petals . . . the gray dove . . .

THE LONESOME GREEN APPLE

There was a little green apple
That had lasted over winter.
He had one leaf . . .
In spite of that he was lonesome.
He wondered what he could do
When the blossoms were all around him,
But one day he saw something!
Petals were falling, faces were looking out,
Shapes like his were coming in the buds;
Then he said:
"If I hold on

There will be a tree-full,
and I shall know more than any of them!"

I AM

I am willowy boughs
For coolness;
I am gold-finch wings
For darkness;
I am a little grape
Thinking of September,
I am a very small violet
Thinking of May.

MUSHROOM SONG

Oh little mushrooms with brown faces underneath
And bare white heads,
You think of summer and you think of song . . .
Why don't you think of me
In my little white bed
In the night?
You think only of your singsong and your dances,
Following your leader round and round,
You think only of the grass
And the green apples and leaves
Dropping out of the blue . . .
Why don't you think of me asleep
In my little white bed?
The wind thinks of me,
Brown-white dancers!

You forget,
But the wind remembers.

THE APPLE-JELLY-FISH-TREE

Down in the depths of the sea
Grew the Apple-Jelly-Fish-Tree.
It was named by a queer old robber
And his mates three.

I watched it for a second,
I watched it for a day.
It did not change color
For its colors stay.

It was as red, as yellow, as white, as blue
As gold and stones with the light through!

I watched it long and long
Till a flying sunfish
Swam through its branches.
He had opal wings
And a sapphire tail.

No wonder robbers like to stay
Where fish so shining come to play!

THREE LOVES

Angel-love,
Fairy-love,
Wave-love,
Which will you choose?
Angel-love . . . golden-yellow and far white . . .
Fairy-love . . . golden yellow and green . . .
Wave-love . . . scarlet and azure blue . . .
Which will you choose?

I will keep them in a box
Locked with a twisted key.
I will give them to people who need love,
I will let them choose.
Fairy-love blows away like leaves.
Angels I know little about.
For myself I choose wave-love
Because of the wind and the sea and my heart.

THE FIELD OF WONDER

What could be more wonderful
Than the place where I walk sometimes?
Swaying like trees in rain . . .
Swaying like trees in sunshine
When breezes stir nothing but happiness . . .
What could be more lovely?
I walk in the Field of Wonder

Where colors come to be;
I stare at the sky . . .
I feel myself lifting on the wind
As the swallows lift and blow upward . . .
I see colors fade out, they die away . . .
I blow across a cloud . . . I am lifted . . .
How can I change again into a little girl
When wings are in my feeling of gladness?
This is strange to know
On a summer day at noon,
This is a wild new joy
When summer is over.
The scarlet of three maple trees
Will guide me home,
Oh mother my dear!
Fear nothing: I will come home
Before snow falls!

MOON DOVES

The moon has a dove-cote safe and small,
Hid in the velvet sky:
The doves are her companions sweet;
She has no others.
Moon doves on the wing are white
As a valley of stars,
When they fly, there is shining
Like a golden river.
I see so many whirling away and away,
How can they get home again?

The moon is calm and never wears an anxious look,
She goes on smiling.
I hear so many doves along the sky
How will her dove-cote hold them?
The moon says not one word to me;
She lets me wonder.

I WENT TO SEA

I WENT to sea in a glass-bottomed boat
And found that the loveliest shells of all
Are hidden below in valleys of sand.
I saw coral and sponge and weed
And bubbles like jewels dangling.
I saw a creature with eyes of mist
Go by slowly.
Star-fish fingers held the water . . .
Let it go again . . .
I saw little fish, the children of the sea;
They were gay and busy.
I wanted the sea-weed purple; I wanted the shells;
I wanted a little fish to hold in my hands;
I wanted the big fish to stop wandering about,
And tell me all they knew . . .
I have come back safe and dry
And know no more secrets
Than yesterday!

THREE THOUGHTS OF MY HEART

As I was straying by the forest brook
I heard my heart speak to me:
Listen; said my heart,
I have three thoughts for you . . .
a thought of clouds,
A thought of birds,
A thought of flowers.

I sat upon a cushion of moss,
Listening,
Where the light played, and the green shadows:
What would you do . . . I asked my heart . . .
If you were a floating ship of the sky . . .
If you were a peering bird . . .
If you were a wild geranium?

And my heart made answer:
That is what I wonder and wonder!
After all it is life I love,
After all I am a living thing,
After all I am the heart of you . . .
I am content!

SNOW-CAPPED MOUNTAIN

Snow-capped mountain, so white, so tall,
The whole sea
Must stand behind you!

Snow-capped mountain, with the wind on your forehead,
Do you hold the eagles' nests?

Proud thing,
You shine like a lily,
Yet with a different whiteness;
I should not dare to venture
Up your slippery towers,
For I am thinking you lean too far
Over the Edge of the World!

THE BROOK AND ITS CHILDREN

"O brook, running down your mossy way,
I hear only your voice
And the murmuring fir-trees;
Where are your children?
Where are the magic stones, your children?"

The brook answered me sweetly,
"I left them on the Alp,
In steep fields.

They were trying to hold me back,
To keep me from this shady path of happiness;
But I went onward day by day
Until they got used to seeing me pass.
Now, they stand there in an enchantment
On the mountain-side,
While I travel fields of elm and poplar."

BIRD OF PARADISE

I was walking in a meadow of Paradise
When I heard a singing
Far away and sweet
Like a Roman harp,
Sweet and murmurous
Like the wind,
Far and soft
Like the fir trees.

It will not change a song
If the bird has a golden crest;
No feathers of blue and rose-red
Could make a song.
I have known in my dreaming
A gray bird that sang
While all the fields listened!
The Bird of Paradise is like flowers of many trees
Blooming on one:
I saw him in the meadow,
But it was the gray bird I heard singing
Beyond and far.

SHINY BROOK

Oh, shiny brook,
I watch you on your way to the sea,
And see little faces peering up
Out of the water . . .
Water-fairies
Strange smiles and questions.
They are your pebbles sweet,
Golden with foam of the sun,
Blue with foam of the sky.
I know their way of speaking,
Of talking to each other:
I hear them telling secrets
About green moss, about fish that get lost.
And how I am sitting on a big stone
Getting my feet wet in Shiny Brook
To watch their surprising ways!

HILLS

The hills are going somewhere;
They have been on the way a long time.
They are like camels in a line
But they move more slowly.
Sometimes at sunset they carry silks,
But most of the time silver birch trees,
Heavy rocks, heavy trees, gold leaves

On heavy branches till they are aching . . .
Birches like silver bars they can hardly lift
With grass so thick about their feet to hinder . . .
They have not gone far
In the time I've watched them . . .

ADVENTURE

I went slowly through the wood of shadows,
Thinking always I should meet some one:
There was no one.

I found a hollow
Sweet to rest in all night long:
I did not stay.

I came out beyond the trees
To the moaning sea.
Over the sea swam a cloud the outline of a ship:
What if that ship held my adventure
Under its sails?

Come quickly to me, come quickly,
I am waiting.
I am here on the sand;
Sail close!
I want to go over the waves . . .
The sand holds me back.
Oh adventure, if you belong to me,
Don't blow away down the sky!

FAIRIES

I cannot see fairies.
I dream them.
There is no fairy can hide from me;
I keep on dreaming till I find him:
There you are, Primrose! I see you, Black Wing!

HUMMING-BIRD

Why do you stand on the air
And no sun shining?
How can you hold yourself so still
On raindrops sliding?
They change and fall, they are not steady,
But you do not know they are gone.
Is there a silver wire
I cannot see?
Is the wind your perch?
Raindrops slide down your little shoulders . . .
They do not wet you:
I think you are not real
In your green feathers!
You are not a humming-bird at all
Standing on air above the garden!
I dreamed you the way I dream fairies,
Or the flower I lost yesterday!

BLUE GRASS

Blue grass flowering in the field,
You are my heart's content.
It is not only through the day I see you,
But in dreams at night
When you trudge up the hill
Along the forest,
As I do!
You are small to shine so,
Nobody speaks of you much,
Because of daisies and such summer blooms.
When you wonder why I like you
It makes me wonder too!
Maybe I remember when you grew high
Like a tree above my head,
Because I was a fairy.

ENVOY

If I am happy, and you,
And there are things to do,
It seems to be the reason
Of this world!

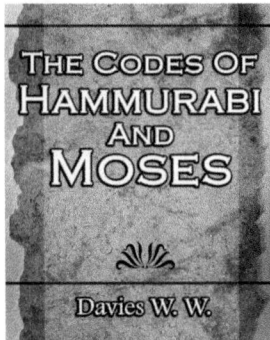

The Codes Of Hammurabi And Moses
W. W. Davies

QTY

The discovery of the Hammurabi Code is one of the greatest achievements of archaeology, and is of paramount interest, not only to the student of the Bible, but also to all those interested in ancient history...

Religion   ISBN: *1-59462-338-4*   Pages:132
MSRP $12.95

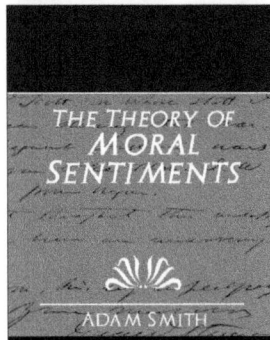

The Theory of Moral Sentiments
Adam Smith

QTY

This work from 1749. contains original theories of conscience amd moral judgment and it is the foundation for systemof morals.

Philosophy   ISBN: *1-59462-777-0*   Pages:536
MSRP $19.95

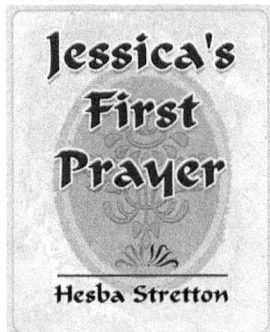

Jessica's First Prayer
Hesba Stretton

QTY

In a screened and secluded corner of one of the many railway-bridges which span the streets of London there could be seen a few years ago, from five o'clock every morning until half past eight, a tidily set-out coffee-stall, consisting of a trestle and board, upon which stood two large tin cans, with a small fire of charcoal burning under each so as to keep the coffee boiling during the early hours of the morning when the work-people were thronging into the city on their way to their daily toil...

Pages:84

Childrens   ISBN: *1-59462-373-2*   MSRP $9.95

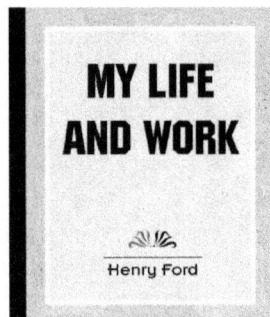

My Life and Work
Henry Ford

QTY

Henry Ford revolutionized the world with his implementation of mass production for the Model T automobile. Gain valuable business insight into his life and work with his own auto-biography... "We have only started on our development of our country we have not as yet, with all our talk of wonderful progress, done more than scratch the surface. The progress has been wonderful enough but..."

Pages:300

Biographies/   ISBN: *1-59462-198-5*   MSRP $21.95

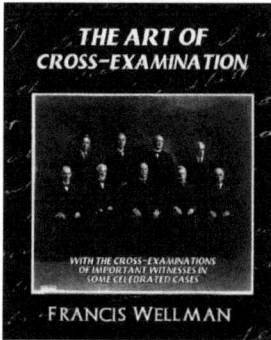

The Art of Cross-Examination
Francis Wellman

QTY

I presume it is the experience of every author, after his first book is published upon an important subject, to be almost overwhelmed with a wealth of ideas and illustrations which could readily have been included in his book, and which to his own mind, at least, seem to make a second edition inevitable. Such certainly was the case with me; and when the first edition had reached its sixth impression in five months, I rejoiced to learn that it seemed to my publishers that the book had met with a sufficiently favorable reception to justify a second and considerably enlarged edition. ..

Reference   **ISBN: *1-59462-647-2***

Pages:412

MSRP $19.95

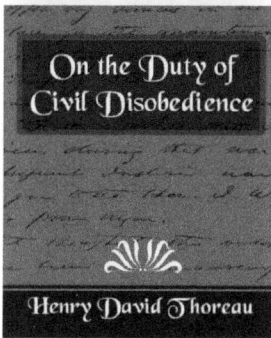

On the Duty of Civil Disobedience
Henry David Thoreau

QTY

Thoreau wrote his famous essay, On the Duty of Civil Disobedience, as a protest against an unjust but popular war and the immoral but popular institution of slave-owning. He did more than write—he declined to pay his taxes, and was hauled off to gaol in consequence. Who can say how much this refusal of his hastened the end of the war and of slavery ?

Law   **ISBN: *1-59462-747-9***

Pages:48

MSRP $7.45

Dream Psychology Psychoanalysis for Beginners
Sigmund Freud

QTY

Sigmund Freud, born Sigismund Schlomo Freud (May 6, 1856 - September 23, 1939), was a Jewish-Austrian neurologist and psychiatrist who co-founded the psychoanalytic school of psychology. Freud is best known for his theories of the unconscious mind, especially involving the mechanism of repression; his redefinition of sexual desire as mobile and directed towards a wide variety of objects; and his therapeutic techniques, especially his understanding of transference in the therapeutic relationship and the presumed value of dreams as sources of insight into unconscious desires.

Psychology   **ISBN: *1-59462-905-6***

Pages:196

MSRP $15.45

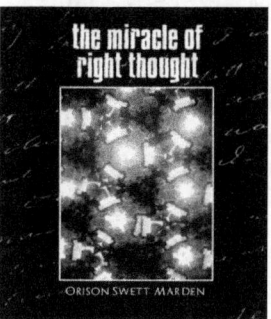

The Miracle of Right Thought
Orison Swett Marden

QTY

Believe with all of your heart that you will do what you were made to do. When the mind has once formed the habit of holding cheerful, happy, prosperous pictures, it will not be easy to form the opposite habit. It does not matter how improbable or how far away this realization may see, or how dark the prospects may be, if we visualize them as best we can, as vividly as possible, hold tenaciously to them and vigorously struggle to attain them, they will gradually become actualized, realized in the life. But a desire, a longing without endeavor, a yearning abandoned or held indifferently will vanish without realization.

Self Help   **ISBN: *1-59462-644-8***

Pages:360

MSRP $25.45

QTY

The Rosicrucian Cosmo-Conception Mystic Christianity by *Max Heindel*   ISBN: *1-59462-188-8*   **$38.95**
The Rosicrucian Cosmo-conception is not dogmatic, neither does it appeal to any other authority than the reason of the student. It is: not controversial, but is: sent forth in the, hope that it may help to clear...   New Age/Religion Pages 646

Abandonment To Divine Providence by *Jean-Pierre de Caussade*   ISBN: *1-59462-228-0*   **$25.95**
"The Rev. Jean Pierre de Caussade was one of the most remarkable spiritual writers of the Society of Jesus in France in the 18th Century. His death took place at Toulouse in 1751. His works have gone through many editions and have been republished...   Inspirational/Religion Pages 400

Mental Chemistry by *Charles Haanel*   ISBN: *1-59462-192-6*   **$23.95**
Mental Chemistry allows the change of material conditions by combining and appropriately utilizing the power of the mind. Much like applied chemistry creates something new and unique out of careful combinations of chemicals the mastery of mental chemistry...   New Age Pages 354

The Letters of Robert Browning and Elizabeth Barret Barrett 1845-1846 vol II   ISBN: *1-59462-193-4*   **$35.95**
by *Robert Browning* and *Elizabeth Barrett*   Biographies Pages 596

Gleanings In Genesis (volume I) by *Arthur W. Pink*   ISBN: *1-59462-130-6*   **$27.45**
Appropriately has Genesis been termed "the seed plot of the Bible" for in it we have, in germ form, almost all of the great doctrines which are afterwards fully developed in the books of Scripture which follow...   Religion/Inspirational Pages 420

The Master Key by *L. W. de Laurence*   ISBN: *1-59462-001-6*   **$30.95**
In no branch of human knowledge has there been a more lively increase of the spirit of research during the past few years than in the study of Psychology, Concentration and Mental Discipline. The requests for authentic lessons in Thought Control, Mental Discipline and...   New Age/Business Pages 422

The Lesser Key Of Solomon Goetia by *L. W. de Laurence*   ISBN: *1-59462-092-X*   **$9.95**
This translation of the first book of the "Lernegton" which is now for the first time made accessible to students of Talismanic Magic was done, after careful collation and edition, from numerous Ancient Manuscripts in Hebrew, Latin, and French...   New Age/Occult Pages 92

Rubaiyat Of Omar Khayyam by *Edward Fitzgerald*   ISBN:*1-59462-332-5*   **$13.95**
Edward Fitzgerald, whom the world has already learned, in spite of his own efforts to remain within the shadow of anonymity, to look upon as one of the rarest poets of the century, was born at Bredfield, in Suffolk, on the 31st of March, 1809. He was the third son of John Purcell...   Music Pages 172

Ancient Law by *Henry Maine*   ISBN: *1-59462-128-4*   **$29.95**
The chief object of the following pages is to indicate some of the earliest ideas of mankind, as they are reflected in Ancient Law, and to point out the relation of those ideas to modern thought.   Religion/History Pages 452

Far-Away Stories by *William J. Locke*   ISBN: *1-59462-129-2*   **$19.45**
"Good wine needs no bush,' but a collection of mixed vintages does. And this book is just such a collection. Some of the stories I do not want to remain buried for ever in the museum files of dead magazine-numbers an author's not unpardonable vanity..."   Fiction Pages 272

Life of David Crockett by *David Crockett*   ISBN: *1-59462-250-7*   **$27.45**
"Colonel David Crockett was one of the most remarkable men of the times in which he lived. Born in humble life, but gifted with a strong will, an indomitable courage, and unremitting perseverance...   Biographies/New Age Pages 424

Lip-Reading by *Edward Nitchie*   ISBN: *1-59462-206-X*   **$25.95**
Edward B. Nitchie, founder of the New York School for the Hard of Hearing, now the Nitchie School of Lip-Reading, Inc, wrote "LIP-READING Principles and Practice". The development and perfecting of this meritorious work on lip-reading was an undertaking...   How-to Pages 400

A Handbook of Suggestive Therapeutics, Applied Hypnotism, Psychic Science   ISBN: *1-59462-214-0*   **$24.95**
by *Henry Munro*   Health/New Age/Health/Self-help Pages 376

A Doll's House: and Two Other Plays by *Henrik Ibsen*   ISBN: *1-59462-112-8*   **$19.95**
Henrik Ibsen created this classic when in revolutionary 1848 Rome. Introducing some striking concepts in playwriting for the realist genre, this play has been studied the world over.   Fiction/Classics/Plays 308

The Light of Asia by *sir Edwin Arnold*   ISBN: *1-59462-204-3*   **$13.95**
In this poetic masterpiece, Edwin Arnold describes the life and teachings of Buddha. The man who was to become known as Buddha to the world was born as Prince Gautama of India but he rejected the worldly riches and abandoned the reigns of power when...   Religion/History/Biographies Pages 170

The Complete Works of Guy de Maupassant by *Guy de Maupassant*   ISBN: *1-59462-157-8*   **$16.95**
"For days and days, nights and nights, I had dreamed of that first kiss which was to consecrate our engagement, and I knew not on what spot I should put my lips..."   Fiction/Classics Pages 240

The Art of Cross-Examination by *Francis L. Wellman*   ISBN: *1-59462-309-0*   **$26.95**
Written by a renowned trial lawyer, Wellman imparts his experience and uses case studies to explain how to use psychology to extract desired information through questioning.   How-to/Science/Reference Pages 408

Answered or Unanswered? by *Louisa Vaughan*   ISBN: *1-59462-248-5*   **$10.95**
Miracles of Faith in China   Religion Pages 112

The Edinburgh Lectures on Mental Science (1909) by *Thomas*   ISBN: *1-59462-008-3*   **$11.95**
This book contains the substance of a course of lectures recently given by the writer in the Queen Street Hall, Edinburgh. Its purpose is to indicate the Natural Principles governing the relation between Mental Action and Material Conditions...   New Age/Psychology Pages 148

Ayesha by *H. Rider Haggard*   ISBN: *1-59462-301-5*   **$24.95**
Verily and indeed it is the unexpected that happens! Probably if there was one person upon the earth from whom the Editor of this, and of a certain previous history, did not expect to hear again...   Classics Pages 380

Ayala's Angel by *Anthony Trollope*   ISBN: *1-59462-352-X*   **$29.95**
The two girls were both pretty, but Lucy who was twenty-one who supposed to be simple and comparatively unattractive, whereas Ayala was credited, as her Bombwhat romantic name might show, with poetic charm and a taste for romance. Ayala when her father died was nineteen...   Fiction Pages 484

The American Commonwealth by *James Bryce*   ISBN: *1-59462-286-8*   **$34.45**
An interpretation of American democratic political theory. It examines political mechanics and society from the perspective of Scotsman James Bryce   Politics Pages 572

Stories of the Pilgrims by *Margaret P. Pumphrey*   ISBN: *1-59462-116-0*   **$17.95**
This book explores pilgrims religious oppression in England as well as their escape to Holland and eventual crossing to America on the Mayflower, and their early days in New England...   History Pages 268

QTY

The Fasting Cure *by Sinclair Upton*　　ISBN: *1-59462-222-1*　**$13.95**
In the Cosmopolitan Magazine for May, 1910, and in the Contemporary Review (London) for April, 1910, I published an article dealing with my experiences in fasting. I have written a great many magazine articles, but never one which attracted so much attention... New Age/Self Help/Health Pages 164

Hebrew Astrology *by Sepharial*　　ISBN: *1-59462-308-2*　**$13.45**
In these days of advanced thinking it is a matter of common observation that we have left many of the old landmarks behind and that we are now pressing forward to greater heights and to a wider horizon than that which represented the mind-content of our progenitors... Astrology Pages 144

Thought Vibration or The Law of Attraction in the Thought World　ISBN: *1-59462-127-6*　**$12.95**
by William Walker Atkinson　　Psychology/Religion Pages 144

Optimism *by Helen Keller*　　ISBN: *1-59462-108-X*　**$15.95**
Helen Keller was blind, deaf, and mute since 19 months old, yet famously learned how to overcome these handicaps, communicate with the world, and spread her lectures promoting optimism. An inspiring read for everyone... Biographies/Inspirational Pages 84

Sara Crewe *by Frances Burnett*　　ISBN: *1-59462-360-0*　**$9.45**
In the first place, Miss Minchin lived in London. Her home was a large, dull, tall one, in a large, dull square, where all the houses were alike, and all the sparrows were alike, and where all the door-knockers made the same heavy sound... Childrens/Classic Pages 88

The Autobiography of Benjamin Franklin *by Benjamin Franklin*　　ISBN: *1-59462-135-7*　**$24.95**
The Autobiography of Benjamin Franklin has probably been more extensively read than any other American historical work, and no other book of its kind has had such ups and downs of fortune. Franklin lived for many years in England, where he was agent... Biographies/History Pages 332

Name	
Email	
Telephone	
Address	
City, State ZIP	

☐ **Credit Card**　　☐ **Check / Money Order**

Credit Card Number	
Expiration Date	
Signature	

Please Mail to: Book Jungle
PO Box 2226
Champaign, IL 61825
or Fax to: 630-214-0564

ORDERING INFORMATION
web: *www.bookjungle.com*
email: *sales@bookjungle.com*
fax: *630-214-0564*
mail: *Book Jungle PO Box 2226 Champaign, IL 61825*
or PayPal *to sales@bookjungle.com*

Please contact us for bulk discounts

DIRECT-ORDER TERMS
20% Discount if You Order Two or More Books
Free Domestic Shipping!
Accepted: Master Card, Visa, Discover, American Express